JAN 1 7 2017

essential careers™

A CAREER AS A
CONSTRUCTION
MANAGER

ANN BYERS

ROSEN
PUBLISHING

NEW YORK

Published in 2016 by The Rosen Publishing Group, Inc.
29 East 21st Street, New York, NY 10010

First Edition

Library of Congress Cataloging-in-Publication Data

Byers, Ann, author.
 A career as a construction manager / Ann Byers. -- First edition.
    pages cm. — (Essential careers)
 Includes bibliographical references and index.
 ISBN 978-1-4994-6209-8 (library bound)
 1. Construction industry—Management—Vocational guidance--Juvenile literature. 2. Building trades—Vocational guidance—Juvenile literature. 3. Construction workers—Juvenile literature. I. Title. II. Series: Essential careers.
 TH438.B87 2016
 624.023—dc23
                              2015024387

Manufactured in the United States of America

contents

INTRO

A construction manager often appears at the job site dressed like all the other construction workers.

DUCTION

J ust a few more minutes of quiet are left. Mike knows the trucks will be rolling through the gate of the work site very soon. City ordinances prohibit loud noise before seven in the morning, so Mike keeps the gate closed until then. Mike takes a last walk alone through the job site. All the building materials remain untouched from yesterday. There has been no theft, no vandalism. The piles of lumber, torn-up ground, and half-finished buildings look a bit scruffy today, but in about ten months the site will be a four-star, 120-room resort hotel with four conference rooms, an outdoor pool, landscaped grounds, and a restaurant.

That is, if Mike can keep everything on schedule. If the plumbers working in Building 4 don't get the gas lines finished soon, the insulators will be behind. The drywall in Building 2 has to be hung today so it can be prepped for the painters who will arrive next week. Weeks ago, a rainstorm set the framers back, but he compensated for lost time by hiring extra crews.

Mike counts the arriving workers and checks the number against his worksheet. The electrical crew is short a couple of hands; he will have to call the sub—the electrical contractor— and get more workers to the site. One of the concrete workers forgot his hard hat, a safety requirement, both for the worker's protection and to prevent legal liability for Mike's company in case of an accident or a fine from government inspectors. Mike gets him a loaner hat before work starts.

Once his crews start work, Mike catches up on the dozen or so phone calls he has to make. The plywood shipment was short, the wiring was the wrong size, and the water truck hadn't arrived. A sewer line has to be rerouted so he needs to discuss the change with a civil engineering firm.

Halfway through his calls, Mike is interrupted by the city building inspector, who pops in occasionally. Today he examines and signs off on the sprinkler system in the main building—another item Mike can check off his long list.

The owner asks Mike for some changes, so he arranges with the architect to redraw the plans. On his way to the trailer that serves as his field office, he spots a roofer with his safety harness unhooked. Sometimes Mike feels his job is a little like herding cats—riding some of the workers, keeping the different crews stacked so there is no down time, and translating drawings from paper specs to slabs of concrete and bricks and mortar.

Mike is the link between architect and carpenter, engineer and welder, designer and craftsman. He listens to complaints and solves problems. He sees the big picture and the little details. Hard as it is, he loves his job as construction manager.

chapter 1

JACK (OR JILL) OF MANY TRADES

The job of a construction manager (CM) is a multi-faceted one. To understand what a CM does, consider the two parts of the job title: construction and manager. First, let's look at the "construction" part; a CM works in the construction industry, in the building trades.

CONSTRUCTION: A BIG FIELD

The construction industry itself is complex. It is made up of two fields, or sectors, with subsectors. The two major divisions are residential and nonresidential. The residential sector is concerned with building all kinds of homes, from small, single-family houses to large, lavish residences. Residential building may be new construction or may entail renovations, or remodels, of existing buildings. Residential construction can mean adding a room to a family home, repairing a house damaged by fire or flood, or building a brand-new high-rise condominium.

The nonresidential sector has at least three subsectors: commercial and institutional, industrial, and engineering. Commercial buildings are those in which business takes place: offices, stores, warehouses, and hotels. They may be single buildings or huge complexes like mega malls, sprawling resorts, or giant skyscrapers. The institutional subsector includes government buildings such as schools, libraries, police stations, and city halls. It also includes privately owned structures that serve the public, like museums, churches, and hospitals. Sports stadiums, recreational centers, and amusement parks belong in the institutional subsector.

Some commercial construction projects are designed for either stores or offices, and some are mixed use, such as this building with both retail and office space.

Industrial construction is concerned with manufacturing and energy. Workers in this subsector build and renovate large facilities such as mills, refineries, and power plants, as well as dams and offshore drilling platforms. These heavy industry projects are similar to those in the engineering construction subsector.

Engineering construction involves roads, bridges, tunnels, railways and mass transit systems, airports, water treatment facilities, and other structures needed for essential services. Construction projects are not always buildings.

MANAGING: A BIG RESPONSIBILITY

As you can see, construction is a very big field. The management part of the CM's job is equally big. CMs are responsible for entire projects from top to bottom and start to finish. A project often involves at least four stages: design (planning the project), procurement (getting everything needed to complete the project), construction (the nitty-gritty work of building), and post-construction (wrapping up the loose ends).

Some projects are so large or have so many parts that they have to be divided into subprojects. In

Builders must consult the architect's plans several times as they complete their projects. Their tools may include a calculator and a small computer.

that case, each subproject has a construction manager or superintendent skilled in one particular aspect of construction. For example, different CMs may be in charge of preparing the construction site; putting in the sewage system; laying the foundation and constructing the building; installing the piping, wiring, and other items needed for the building to function; and applying paint, stucco, stonework, and other finishing touches. They may be called superintendents rather than CMs, but their subprojects can be very large, and they are responsible for every task and every phase of those subprojects.

Managing a project means taking responsibility for everything about the project—the people, the materials, the money, how long it takes, and its quality.

MANAGING PEOPLE

CMs work with three different types of people in distinctly different ways. First is the client. The client is the owner, the person or company that wants the project built and is paying for it. CMs report to the client.

Many CMs are self-employed contractors, and they work on small projects directly for the client. On large projects, however, the clients hire construction companies, and the CM works for the construction company. That means the CM is responsible to two different people at the same time: the project owner, or client, and the owner of the construction company, his or her actual boss.

Having two bosses can be challenging. What if the client wants to make a change the construction company owner says cannot be done? What if the construction company can't get the materials the client insists on? The CM has to find ways to please both bosses.

Second, CMs work with professionals not directly involved with the physical, hands-on aspects of the building process.

PLANNING HELPS

Construction managers use calendars, charts, and graphs to help them plan their projects. These tools let them see the order they need to follow. Some types of charts and graphs allow them to see processes that overlap, or happen at the same time.

Processes may be split up according to different building sections, or different types of work. A chart may show how windows and electrical wiring, for example, may be installed simultaneously. Visual aids are a great way for some people to track what workers and resources need to be deployed at certain times, rather than trying to juggle all these elements off the top of one's head.

Managers might use construction schedules as simple as a calendar or might employ complex charts, graphs, and other visual tools to plan a project.

Many companies produce their own internal documents that help project managers track schedules. Others buy expensive software that can truly help plan and integrate all the different parts of projects, including payroll, deadlines, cost estimates, and much more.

Few projects adhere exactly to the schedules and plans a manager tries to impose on them. Even if some deadlines are set in stone, a good manager must be willing to be flexible with many of the processes involved.

Some of the professionals are the architects and engineers that plan and design the project. Sometimes the plans cannot be carried out in real life, and the CM and the professional planner have to work together to adjust for real-life conditions. CMs also work with surveyors, cost estimators, and other construction managers. One very important professional on every project is the inspector. The building or construction inspector checks to see that everything about the project conforms to city, state, and national codes and regulations.

Third are the tradespeople. Building just one house demands many different kinds of skilled tradespeople. These can include concrete workers, bricklayers, framers, plasterers, sheet-metal workers, finish carpenters, roofers, electricians, HVAC (heating, ventilation, and air-conditioning) installers, plumbers, tile setters, painters, and more. CMs hire, fire, and manage these tradespeople. A CM working as a general contractor on a small job may work directly with them, but on larger projects CMs usually hire subcontractors. CMs make sure the workers are properly equipped and are doing their jobs correctly and safely.

Professionals and tradespeople make agreements with the client or the construction company about what they will do, how they will do it, and what they will be paid. CMs are responsible for writing and negotiating the details of very detailed and specific contracts.

Written plans and illustrations are valuable tools that are used by a construction manager to transform an idea on paper into a real-life structure.

MANAGING MATERIALS, MONEY, AND TIME

Every construction project has plenty of materials, supplies, and equipment. All of it has to be procured—either purchased

or rented. Once on the site, everything must be stored safely. It has to be inventoried and tracked: How much was received? How much was used? What was done with the leftover materials? The CM keeps careful records of everything on the job site.

Tracking materials for a project helps CMs manage money, a responsibility that begins long before anything arrives on site. When the project is still in the design stage, CMs must estimate costs for every part of the project and prepare budgets. During construction, they control what is spent and make reports to their bosses.

Timeliness is essential for any building project. Everything has to be scheduled: when equipment is needed, delivery of materials and supplies, and start times for different phases of the project. If one item or one work crew is late, everything behind it is delayed. For example, if the drywallers take too long to finish their job, the

CMs consult weather agencies to predict delays, such as cranes having to sit idle in a rainstorm. They figure these predictions into their time and cost estimates for the job.

painters cannot start; if the painters fall behind, the tile setters cannot install the flooring on schedule. In construction, as in many businesses, time is money, and lost time is lost money. The painters may arrive on time but cannot begin their work because of the drywallers' delay. Nevertheless, they must be paid even though there is no work for them yet. CMs schedule the entire job and set deadlines before construction begins; they also draw up schedules for each week and each day. They stay on top of all the crews to keep everyone on track.

The best schedule can be thrown off by bad weather, equipment breakdowns, and other unforeseen circumstances. CMs often add a little time to the project schedule to cover these surprises. Sometimes they have to scramble to find ways to make up the lost time.

Finishing the project on time is very important. Construction companies sign contracts with clients to finish by a certain date and for a certain amount of money. When a client announces plans for a project, construction companies compete for the job in a bidding process. This means the companies bid on the project and the client often awards the job to the contractor who can do the job at the lowest reasonable price and in the least amount of time. Hence, the amount of leeway a company has can be very tight indeed. The companies can be charged thousands of dollars for every day they are late in completing the project. That is one reason the job of construction manager is so important in terms of time and money.

chapter 2

ONE CAREER, THREE LADDERS

The position of construction manager is not an entry-level job. It is a higher rung on a career ladder. Actually, three different career paths, or ladders, can take you from high school to the job of CM.

As we saw in the last chapter, a CM has to have two kinds of skills: construction skills and management skills. Two of the career ladders are heavy on the construction skills and one emphasizes managerial skills, but all three can lead to a CM position. We'll call them the on-the-job, vocational, and university ladders.

THREE LADDERS

Construction often involves learning on the job. The on-the-job ladder begins with learning a specific building craft: framing, roofing, or hanging drywall, for example. You learn the skills by working in the trade; no formal schooling is necessary. You move up this ladder, climbing to more responsible positions and making more money, through apprenticeship. An apprentice is someone who works under an experienced craftsperson who helps the apprentice get better at the craft. Some apprenticeships are formal and some just happen.

You can climb higher to become a professional in any particular craft. A professional is certified by an organization that

For this sixth-grader, taking woodworking classes in school helps him learn techniques, develop skills, and get a feel for the trade.

is recognized as upholding the standards of the specific craft. People on this ladder who show an interest or proficiency in management can become CMs.

The vocational ladder requires some education after high school, usually from a community college, a technical school, or an apprenticeship program. This formal training enables tradesmen and tradeswomen to move quickly into supervisory positions on the work site, such as forepersons or crew leaders. These are positions in which they can develop management abilities that will help them eventually become CMs. The schooling also exposes them to areas of construction that are not in the building crafts, such as cost estimating, safety, and inspection. Jobs in these areas can also lead to CM positions.

One path leads directly to construction management. On the university path, students learn both construction and management. Many people who already have some knowledge of the building crafts choose this path. With a four-year college degree, they may be able to get jobs as CMs with big companies on large projects. They may actually have little experience building anything themselves but know a great deal about construction and are good at managing. They can start as CMs and advance to the very top of the ladder. Let's look at some of the rungs on that ladder.

SUPERVISORY RUNGS

A craftsperson good at his or her trade can advance to the position of foreperson or crew leader. A crew is a team of people all in one trade—all roofers, HVAC technicians, or solar panel installers, for example. Forepersons oversee the people and manage the work of their crew. This is a rung between craftsperson and manager. Forepersons are craftspeople, very skilled in their trade, and they often work alongside the other people on the crew. They have some responsibility over who does what and when. But they are not responsible for managing time or money. They are the ones who provide the on-the-job training to the people under them. A foreperson does not need college or vocational training; he or she needs lots of hands-on experience in the particular trade, whether it be as an electrician, carpenter, or any other craftsperson.

A rung above the foreperson is superintendent. Superintendents are in charge of more than one crew. Sometimes they manage an entire site. They supervise the forepersons much like the forepersons direct their crews. They are not responsible for the overall schedule of the project, but they may

THREE LADDERS TO CONSTRUCTION MANAGEMENT

Each of these three paths can lead to a job as a construction manager . . . and beyond.

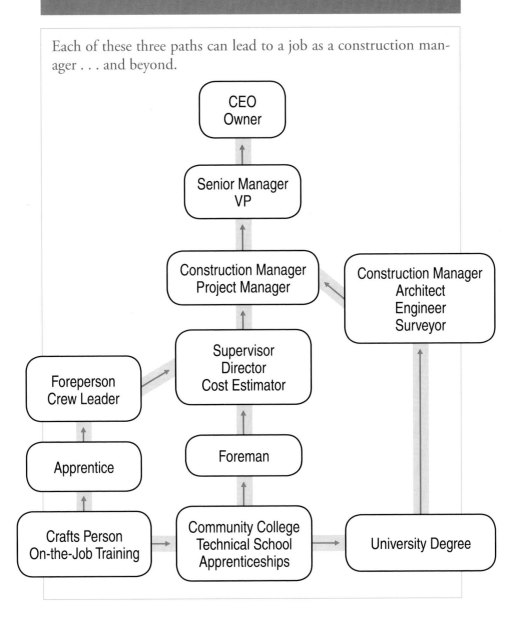

make decisions about the day-to-day scheduling and placement of crews. Superintendents are generally craftspeople with some supervisory training. They might get that training in a vocational program at a junior college or technical school.

MANAGEMENT RUNGS

The difference between a management job and a supervisory job in construction is in the level of responsibility and decision making. Managers are generally responsible for coordinating and making decisions about a number of tasks. In construction, supervisory jobs all have to do with overseeing people; management jobs have an extra layer of responsibility because they deal with managing things and processes.

The cost estimator, for example, is a money manager. Large projects use cost estimators to figure out how much money will be needed to complete a project. They look at architects' plans to see what materials, equipment, and labor the job will require. Then they gather

quotes from suppliers and subcontractors who want to provide the products and services. These quotes help decision makers ascertain what expenses are reasonable. They draw up budgets based on these quotes.

These surveyors are matching what they see at the site with the measurements and features depicted on their blueprints.

Schedulers are the time managers for large projects. They make decisions about the timing and the flow of materials and people. They use charts and computer programs to schedule work and adjust for delays. They personally do not keep a project on schedule, but when it gets behind, they are the ones who figure out what has to be done to get it back on track.

Construction companies that have several projects going at the same time may employ safety managers. Safety managers oversee practices on job sites. They make sure workers are following all the state and federal rules about working safely. Before a job begins, they study the plans and decide what is needed to keep everyone safe. They know who should wear goggles and what noise levels are potentially damaging to workers' hearing, and hence when they should wear protective gear. They plan how chemicals and supplies will be stored and what signs will be posted. When the project is underway, the safety manager visits the site to ensure that conditions remain safe.

Some large companies and big projects have an operations manager, planners, and project coordinators who manage different aspects of construction projects. Most of the management rungs below CM are found only in large companies. They all require some formal training; many employers prefer or require people in management positions to have bachelor's degrees.

ENGINEERING RUNGS

A bachelor's degree or higher is also needed for engineering jobs. These are neither supervisory nor management positions; they are design jobs. Engineers create the pictures and the technical plans for the building project. On one rung of the engineering ladder are architects, who design and draw the plans for buildings and other structures. On another rung are surveyors, who measure and report on the features of land. Civil engineers develop plans for roads, bridges, and other large

This six-lane suspension bridge connecting the island city of Cádiz to the Spanish mainland was an eight-year project. It is one of the tallest and longest bridges in the world.

structures. Building service engineers, also called architectural or building engineers, design the electrical and mechanical systems that provide services in the buildings, such as heating and lighting systems, elevators, and security systems.

Even though engineers do not construct or manage, they are on the construction management ladder. They do not necessarily want to become CMs, but some of the people who work with them as assistants or technicians may. People working in an engineering company or an architectural firm gain some knowledge about construction. They learn to read and draw blueprints, they understand building codes, and they learn about building materials and procedures. If they have some management abilities, they may choose to pursue a career in construction management.

BEYOND CONSTRUCTION MANAGER

Every construction project does not include every one of the jobs described in this section. Some small projects may use only craftspeople and forepersons. Some multiyear projects may employ people in all these positions. Whatever supervisors, managers, and engineers work on a job, the CM interacts with every one.

Being a CM is often exciting and rewarding, but it is not the top of the career ladder. CMs can remain on their rung and make a comfortable living, or they can move higher. The next step up is to become a project manager. On a very large project, the CM may manage a portion of the project, and a project manager is in charge of the entire project. A CM works on site, overseeing the activities that take place there. A project manager, however, usually works in an office, overseeing operations by integrating and analyzing the reports of the CMs and others beneath him or her.

CMs who are general contractors or work in small

FROM HOUSING REMODELS TO POWER PLANTS

Ryan Nellis learned to swing a hammer as a kid, helping his dad on projects around the house. When he was in high school, he worked during the summer as a laborer on construction sites. In college, he joined a rough carpentry crew, building houses. Those early experiences gave him a good feel for the construction industry, and he became interested in the management aspects. So he pursued a bachelor's degree in construction management. While he was still in college, an industrial contractor hired him to work on projects using concrete and steel.

Ten years later, Nellis is overseeing a $90 million renovation of a science center at Eastern Michigan University. Over the years, he worked as a construction project engineer and helped build, among many other things, steel mills, petroleum refining facilities, and a power plant. What he particularly likes about his job as a construction manager is the variety it offers.

"Every day is different," he told the website My Footpath, "and every new project presents a new set of challenges."

Any type of housing building or repair, including home improvement projects, develops skills and builds experience for a career in construction.

companies may need to progress to larger companies or projects in order to gain enough experience and confidence to become project managers. Those who became CMs through on-the-job training will need to earn a college degree in order to be hired as project managers.

Some project managers climb higher still. Some become operations managers, general managers, vice presidents, or presidents of their companies. Others prefer the construction aspect of their job to the management responsibilities and pursue high-level engineering careers. Whichever path, whichever ladder, a career as a CM offers many possibilities.

chapter 3

GREEN-COLLAR CONSTRUCTION MANAGERS

Among the many options for careers in construction management are positions in green building. "Green building" is a term for construction that is environmentally friendly. It is also called sustainable building because it preserves, or sustains, natural resources. More and more owners and construction companies are using sustainable building practices in their projects. Government at all levels has been encouraging these practices through tax incentives and laws, while owners and contractors have begun to recognize that green building is good not only for the environment but for their bottom line as well.

The U.S. Green Building Council has established standards that enable builders to measure how green, or environmentally friendly, their projects are. The measurement system is called Leadership in Energy and Environmental Design, or LEED. Builders earn LEED points for different parts of the construction process if they can show they use green materials and techniques. If a project receives enough points, it is ranked by LEED as certified, silver, gold, or platinum. Many clients want their projects to have a high LEED ranking, and the CM is the person responsible for getting that rank.

Green building is different from other types of construction in three important ways: the materials used, the way energy and water are managed, and the way waste is managed during the building and disposed of afterward. These differences mean some additional responsibilities for CMs.

MANAGING GREEN MATERIALS

To sustain the environment, green builders use materials that are renewable—that nature can make again. Lumber comes from trees, and all trees can grow back under the right conditions. But some grow back faster than others. An oak tree takes one hundred twenty years to reach maturity, a pine tree thirty to fifty years, and bamboo three to seven years. A natural product that can replace itself within ten years or less is considered a rapidly renewable resource. Green CMs look for rapidly renewable building materials.

In addition to renewable products, recycled materials are environmentally friendly. CMs sometimes use bricks, posts, and other items salvaged from other building projects. They also use products made from recycled items, such as bottlestone countertops, made from ground pieces of discarded glass.

How green a particular item

is—and therefore how many LEED points its use can receive— is also determined by how far from the construction site it originated. Building products are transported by trucks to the site, and trucks burn diesel fuel, which is not friendly to the

To be certified "green," lumber must come from a forest in which all plants and animals are protected, all trees in a tract are not removed, and pesticides are not used.

environment. So CMs try to find materials that are no farther than 500 miles (about 800 kilometers) from where they will be used.

CMs have to document that the materials they purchase meet the standards for "greenness" that earn LEED points. For lumber, that means having a "chain of custody," a certificate that tracks each board's history, proving that it was grown, cut, maintained, and shipped in an environmentally friendly way. For manufactured products such as linoleum or insulation, they must estimate and prove what percent of the products are made up of renewable or recycled materials. CMs have to document how far the materials traveled. As you can see, a great deal of managing materials for green projects requires math skills and careful attention to detail. To earn LEED points, CMs can even document how much of their reporting is done on recycled paper.

MANAGING ENERGY AND WATER

Because so much energy in buildings comes from nonrenewable sources (coal, oil, and natural gas), green builders are also dedicated to reducing energy use. Reducing energy use in green buildings is achieved largely by decisions made in the design phase. Engineers and architects determine in what directions buildings will face, where windows will be, and where to plant shade trees and other greenery. These are factors that affect how much natural energy can be used for heating, cooling, and lighting. Engineers select the appropriate heating and cooling systems and an assortment of energy conservation features. The CM's job is the same as it would be for a traditional construction site: to simply carry out the engineers' plans.

Unlike on a traditional site, however, CMs on some green projects manage energy in the building processes. Some large projects generate their own energy on the site to run the

The solar panels on this house are only one of its energy conservation measures. The orientation of the building, the trees, and the windows all figure in energy efficiency.

construction equipment. They create energy from renewable resources, like the sun, wind, geothermal energy (energy from subterranean rock and water), running water and tidal power, and other sources. The CM manages the production, storage, and use of this energy during the construction phase.

Like energy, water is a big concern for sustainable builders. Water is a renewable resource, but it is not being renewed. According to the 2005 *LEED for New Construction Reference Guide*, the United States uses 3.7 billion gallons (14 trillion liters) more water every year than it puts back into the environment. Green builders give much thought to reducing water

To be certified "green," insulation such as these mineral wood panels must be manufactured with local, partially recycled materials within 500 miles (800 km) of where it is installed.

use. As with energy conservation, features that help with water conservation are figured out in the design phase. The architects and engineers integrate these features into their plans, and the CM makes sure the plans are followed.

The one conservation area that falls squarely on the shoulders of the CM on a green project is waste management. A construction project creates a lot of waste—2.5 pounds of solid waste per square foot of finished floor space, according to the 2007 *LEED for New Construction Reference Guide*. Most of that waste can be recycled. Builders at other sites might be able to use lumber, pipes, cabinets, light fixtures, tile, and similar

BEYOND GREEN

Environmentally conscious builders are always looking for new ways to conserve energy. Fostering this kind of innovation is one reason LEED standards were established. A LEED gold-rated building uses 25 percent less energy than a traditional building. New technologies are producing even greater energy savings, with even greater yields expected in the future.

Some of these technologies are used in a design called Passive House. Developed in Germany, Passive House (Passivhaus, in the original German) is a design standard that can reduce the amount of energy used for heating and cooling a building by as much as 90 percent. A structure built to this standard is air-tight and super insulated, and it uses a ventilation system that balances the heat and moisture in the air. Passive House buildings maintain stable temperatures and excellent air quality around the clock.

The standard is not just for residences; the Raiffeisen-Holding Hochhaus office tower in Vienna, Austria, is a skyscraper certified as meeting the Passive House standard. Its energy consumption is 80 percent less than for any other building of its size.

items. Leftover chunks of concrete and asphalt can be crushed, mixed with cement, and used to pave another site. Shingles, broken glass, paneling, and pieces of drywall can all be turned into new products. Even the cardboard boxes supplies come in can be recycled.

CMs develop waste management plans before construction begins. They study the architect's plans and get an idea of what kind of waste to expect. They figure out what can be reused on the job and what can be recycled. A number of businesses recycle products, and the CM has to contact several to find out what items they accept. How will they get the waste to the recycling processers? Will the recyclers pick up the materials or does the CM need to assign vehicles and drivers to get the waste to them? Bins for collecting the unused items have to be set up on the job site—different containers for different kinds of

To reuse scraps of construction materials and packaging, green builders usually have bins for collecting wood, metal, concrete, and cardboard waste for recycling.

materials. The CMs have to label the bins clearly and explain the plan to all the workers.

Once construction begins, CMs make sure the workers are following the waste management plan. The CM may have to

check the collection bins every day to see that the right items have been put in the correct containers. A recycler that processes concrete may not accept waste that has pieces of wood mixed in. The CM may also need to check the garbage regularly to retrieve reusable items that workers have thrown away. They need to schedule pickup or delivery of the items ahead of time, before the bins are filled completely. To score LEED points and show their bosses how much money they have saved by recycling, they make sure to get very detailed receipts.

Extensive recordkeeping and documentation are an essential part of a CM's job. So are time management, budgeting, contracts, safety, and quality control. Planning, hiring, supervising, and training are major elements of the CM's job description. Such a multifaceted job demands a person with diverse interests and abilities.

chapter 4

IS THIS JOB FOR ME?

Part builder, part manager . . . does this sound like a job you would like? Prospective candidates should explore what it takes to do well on the job and some of the things construction managers say they like and dislike about the work. First, do you have what it takes to be a good CM?

PERSONAL TRAITS

The construction part of the CM position can be physically demanding; are you willing to work hard for long hours, constantly on your feet? Even if a CM mostly manages others, there are often times he or she will need to be hands-on with equipment or supplies, whether to help out on site or show others the ropes.

You will need to know about every aspect of your particular type of construction; are you willing to learn? Taking classes and even getting a college degree are part of the territory. Once you are on the job, it may take several years to climb to the CM rung on the ladder; are you willing to put in the time?

The management part of the job means you will be working with many other people. How well do you get along with others? You will have to deal with architects, engineers, and inspectors, and the job site may have professional craftspeople, semiskilled laborers, and high school kids trying to break into

Construction managers work with people. They have to be able to explain plans, help others know what to do, and encourage them to do it well.

the field. Can you see the value of each one and treat them all with respect?

What about if they are not doing a good job? CMs sometimes have to tell workers to do things they don't want to do or reprimand someone for not following instructions. At times they have to fire people. Do you think you can confront people in uncomfortable situations like these? Can you do so firmly yet kindly?

CMs are in charge of entire sites and big projects. They have to be leaders. They can't wait around for someone to tell them what to do; they must be self-starters. With many decisions to make daily, they also need to be confident and self-assured. Do you take the initiative when something needs to be done? Do other people sometimes look to you for leadership? You may have what it takes to do the managerial part of a CM's job.

Another important personal trait for a CM to have is flexibility. If you get flustered when something unexpected interrupts your plans, this is not the job for you. On any construction site equipment breaks down, materials are the wrong size, accidents happen, and rain falls. CMs are the ones responsible for figuring out what to do when unforeseen problems develop, so they need to be calm under pressure. If you are willing to work and learn, if you enjoy working with others, and if you are a self-confident leader, flexible, and calm, you have the personal traits for construction management.

SKILLS AND ABILITIES

In addition to these personal traits, CMs need certain skills to do their job well. It takes time and experience to fully develop these abilities, but let's look at them and consider whether you might enjoy using these in a full-time position. Can you see yourself growing into these skills?

Many people enter the CM career path through a construction trade. If this is your plan, are you fairly good at building? If you think you want to follow the university track, how are your academic skills? This path requires a lot of math, science, and technology.

CMs are problem solvers. Sometimes what their clients envision or what designers outline on paper is hard to create on the real-life job site. That is a process that a CM must help see through to completion. When circumstances or clients force changes in the project, the CM must decide how to adjust to these. Sometimes prices go up, materials are not available, or vandals steal supplies. Those are all problems the CM must solve as an everyday part of the job. How do you handle problems? Do you get frustrated and give up? Or do you see them as challenges and enjoy looking for solutions? A CM must be able to roll with the punches.

Because CMs are in charge of entire projects, they must be able to multitask. Even on a small construction site, many activities are taking place at the same time. The CM may need to supervise more than one crew, order products, talk with a landscaper, and meet the city inspector, sometimes all in rapid succession. Are you able to keep more than one idea in your head at a time?

Multitasking requires that CMs manage time well. Can you judge how long it will take you to perform certain tasks? Do you turn assignments in on schedule? Are you on time for different events? Do you procrastinate or do you tackle responsibilities right away?

Another important part of the CM's job is being a good communicator. CMs must be able to communicate well in person, over the phone, and in writing. They must ensure that their instructions and requests are clearly understood by employees under them, clients, vendors, and coworkers. They also have to be very organized in their written reports, keeping

Construction tools include not only power tools and other mechanical equipment, but also phones and other mobile technology that keep a manager connected to potentially dozens of individuals daily.

track of what needs to be done, what has been accomplished, what agreements were made, what money was spent, and many other details. If you are a list maker, organization may be a natural ability for you. If not, you can develop this and any other skill you need.

WILL I LIKE THE JOB?

If you have most of the personality traits and abilities described above you will probably make a good construction manager. But will you be happy in the position? Every job has aspects that are enjoyable and facets that may not be particularly pleasant. Let's look at what construction managers say about their work. That will highlight some of the pros and cons of the job.

One positive feature that is mentioned often is the variety of tasks and experiences. Many like the fact that they spend part of their time indoors and part outside. Most enjoy the fact that every workday and every job is different. Even if are unreasonable or demanding.

Another consideration is the fact that the profession is project based. CMs who work for large companies like the fact that each new project is different. But CMs who work for companies with multiple projects sometimes have to move to another city and live there for a year or two to complete a project. Being away from home for extended stretches of time on shorter projects can be trying, especially if a CM has a family. When projects are small, CMs who are general contractors have to keep finding new projects in order to keep working throughout the year.

SALARY AND OUTLOOK

One very big positive for the job of constructive manager is the salary. CMs generally can expect above-average earnings. You can check the U.S. Bureau of Labor Statistics website for current pay ranges. In addition to their salaries, some may receive bonuses if they are able to save money for their bosses on projects. Some may also have the use of a company vehicle. More than half of all CMs in the United States are self-employed; their annual earnings depend on how much business they get.

The U.S. Bureau of Labor Statistics forecasts that the number of construction management jobs will grow faster than the national average of all jobs through the year 2022. Remember, there are many variations of construction manager positions. Some are general contractors working for themselves on small jobs and others are employees of large companies. There are differences in residential, commercial and institutional, industrial, and engineering fields. There are specialties such as new construction, renovations, and green building. New jobs will be available in all these fields.

A growing national and international emphasis on energy and water conservation is influencing the adoption of advanced, environmentally friendly building practices; CMs skilled at implementing these practices will be needed. Many clients and construction companies want CMs with both experience in the trade and a bachelor's degree in construction science, construction management, or civil engineering. That means that getting a job as a CM these days may take some effort.

chapter 5

GETTING THE JOB

A construction manager job is not an entry-level position. But it is attainable with time and effort. Anyone, male or female, with the personal traits and skills described in the last chapter and the willingness to work at it for probably a minimum of five years can become a construction manager. During that time, you can capitalize on your strengths and work on your weaknesses. Getting the job takes a combination of experience and education. One way to obtain experience and education at the same time is through an apprenticeship.

APPRENTICESHIP

An apprenticeship is a structured on-the-job training program. A construction apprentice works in a specific building craft, such as ironworking, masonry, or carpentry. The apprentice learns the craft by working under the guidance and supervision of a tradesperson skilled in that particular craft. The person is a teacher and can often become a mentor. Mentors and apprentices may forge lifelong relationships.

When apprentices have spent enough time working in the trade, have developed a good grasp of its fundamentals, and can demonstrate the necessary skills, they can move up to the next level, which is journeyman. Despite the name, a journeyman is not necessarily a man; women can do equally well in the

Journeymen help people studying to become architects, engineers, project managers, and other construction professionals learn to read and create blueprints and revise them on the jobsite.

construction trades. The next step after journeyman is master craftsperson.

An apprenticeship usually lasts three to five years, depending on the craft. Tile setters and cement masons, for example, have three-year apprenticeships, whereas sheet-metal workers and glaziers take five years to complete an apprenticeship program. Apprentices work at actual construction sites and are paid for their work. They are paid less than journeymen because they are less skilled. As they complete more hours of training and hone their skills, their pay goes up.

In addition to learning on the job, apprentices take classes, often at night. In the classroom they learn about safety, tools, and techniques of the trade. The number of hours in the classroom also varies but typically ranges from 140 to 250 hours per year, although it could be much higher for particular crafts. Once an apprentice has the required number of hours and years in the field and in the classroom, he or she can take a state test to become licensed as a journeyman. After a few more years of experience, a journeyman may take another test to be recognized as a master in the particular craft.

Most apprenticeships do not cost the apprentice anything. Through the Workforce Investment Act, the U.S. Department of Labor gives funds to states to provide job training and to establish standards and practices for that training. Programs that meet the standards and receive the federal funds are called registered apprenticeship programs. Each state gives the money to agencies or groups that create registered apprenticeship programs. The programs might be sponsored and operated by businesses, schools, nonprofit organizations, or professional associations working individually or together. You can find an apprenticeship program in your region by typing "registered apprenticeships" and the name of your city, town, or county in any Internet search engine.

Many trade unions or labor unions, which are associations

THE COLLEGE PATH

Of the three ladders to construction management, Joanna Slominski chose college. Growing up on a farm in northern Minnesota, she knew from childhood that she wanted to have some sort of a physical career in the outdoors. She went to North Dakota State University to study architecture. Before long she realized that she enjoyed the building part of construction more than the drawing aspects. She switched directions and earned a bachelor of science degree in construction engineering. When she graduated she went to work right away for a large construction company, where she has worked for six years. Because she wants to grow professionally, she became LEED certified and is preparing to test to also be a professional engineer. Her current assignment is as construction manager on a renovation project for the thirty-year-old Minnesota Zoo. She is in charge of building a new penguin exhibit, a new bird theater, and a new education space.

Moving up one of the construction management career ladders requires many hours of study and good grades on a series of certification tests.

that enable people to earn bachelor's degrees in construction science, building science, or construction engineering. The programs have courses in project control and management, design, blueprint reading, construction methods and materials, cost estimation, building codes and standards, labor relations, contract administration, and other topics. These degrees, or degrees in architecture or engineering, coupled with experience, are often enough to land a position as an assistant CM or a technician in a large construction company. They prepare you for the next step in the profession, which is certification.

CERTIFICATION

Construction managers do not need to be certified, but some companies will not hire a CM who is not certified. Certification by a professional organization identifies CMs as professionals. It shows they have met very high standards and are very good at what they do. Two national organizations offer CM certification.

The Construction Management Association of America awards the Certified Construction Manager certification. People can test for this certificate if they have forty-eight months' experience as CMs and meet the educational requirement. They can meet the educational requirement in one of three ways: earning a bachelor's degree from an accredited college or university; obtaining an associate's degree plus four years of experience in construction or construction design (in addition to the forty-eight months as a CM); or, barring any formal degree, by having eight years' construction experience in addition to their CM experience.

The American Institute of Constructors offers two levels of certification. The Associate Constructor certification is for people just entering the CM profession. To take the test for this certificate, a person must have either four years of education in construction, four years of experience, or some combination of the two. The eight-hour exam contains three hundred questions on basic construction management topics such as engineering concepts, management concepts, construction materials and methods, cost estimating and control, budgeting, planning, scheduling, safety, and communication. For the second level, Certified Professional Constructor, at least eight years of experience or a combination of experience and education are required. Passing the rigorous test is not the end of the certification process. To maintain their standing as American Institute of Constructors certificated professionals, CMs must take additional classes and seminars every two years.

It may seem a long path from high school graduation to professional construction manager. But every step along the way is potentially exciting and rewarding. The path—and the rewards—can begin even before high school ends.

chapter 6

WHAT CAN I DO NOW?

No matter how far in the future your desired career is, it is never too early to prepare for it. If you have not yet graduated from high school or if you are just beginning college, there are steps you can take right now that will make getting the job of construction manager in a few years easier.

TAKE THE RIGHT CLASSES

Think about the construction skills and knowledge you will need. Remember, CMs must know about every phase of building. Measuring and calculating will be involved, so math, algebra, and geometry classes are crucial. Art classes are good preparation for the architecture and design aspects of construction. Chemistry and physics are excellent prerequisites for engineering and some of the building trades.

Consider also the management skills and knowledge you will need. CMs deal with all kinds of people, so taking a psychology course or two will be helpful. You will be estimating costs and preparing budgets. Beyond basic math, accounting and other business classes would be good choices. Don't forget the importance of language proficiency and communication skills. Some English or writing classes might be useful. CMs write contracts, make bids, give reports, and make presentations. Most of the management tools and many construction

Welding is one of the building trades taught in some high schools. High school teachers often provide personal attention that gives students foundations in safety and proper techniques.

design tools today are digital, so you will need to be comfortable with computer technology.

Many high schools have vocational or technical classes that can provide a head start. You can learn woodworking, drafting, building design, architectural drawing, electrical installation, mechanical construction, and much more. Some trade schools and community colleges give college credit for certain high school courses. The point of taking the right classes is to learn, so of course doing well and getting good grades is important!

While you're getting the fundamentals and a feel for the many different facets of construction, make a point of learning about trends in the construction industry. Companies have switched from paper scheduling to using time-tracking software. Read up on sustainable building, Passive House design, and net-zero construction. Find out how the construction industry is using laser scanners, 3D printers, and drones. You are preparing for CM jobs of tomorrow, so learn all you can about what they will be like.

JOIN A CONSTRUCTION TEAM

One of the best ways to prepare for a career in construction management is to be around construction. If you know anyone in a building trade, ask if you can help out at a construction site. Look on the Internet for summer or part-time entry-level jobs. Talk to a guidance counselor or someone in the career planning office at your school about job openings. When you are unskilled, any job at a building site, even just sweeping up, puts you in a position to learn and to meet people who may be hiring.

Build something as a volunteer. A number of organizations are very happy to have young people help on their building projects, and most provide some training. One of the most well-known, Habitat for Humanity, accepts volunteers as

A CANSTRUCTION PROJECT

Construction is not just about wood, bricks, and concrete. It is about design and problem solving. Teachers at Kearny High School in New Jersey heard about a competition sponsored by the non-profit organization Canstruction. Entrants design and build a large structure from cans of food, and after the competition the cans are donated to food pantries that feed the hungry. The students had to apply planning, engineering, and teamwork skills to construct their entry. They used computer programs to help them calculate dimensions, built scale models, and dealt with a variety of technical issues. One of the design problems was getting enough cans of the right color in the proper places. The students ended up assembling about twenty thousand cans in twenty levels on wooden supports to build a giant globe. The project has been so successful—both in helping students make practical application of the construction skills they are learning, and at replenishing food pantries—that the school has made participation in the contest an annual ritual.

These architects' blueprints determine how their project will look. Engineers take the architects' drawings and determine what has to be done to make the design function properly.

young as fourteen on some projects. These projects usually involve sprucing up houses—painting, landscaping, and making minor repairs. At age sixteen, volunteers can join teams building new homes or making major repairs and renovations. They can learn new skills by working alongside people who know what they are doing.

Habit for Humanity is not the only organization offering volunteer opportunities. The Volunteer Match website keeps track of volunteer openings throughout the United States and lists hundreds of groups looking for volunteers in construction. States, counties, and cities often have volunteer bureaus that connect people with service needs.

If you can't find a volunteer team, why not create one? Look for a need in your community—a neighbor whose house needs painting or whose fence or roof needs repair. Maybe there is a newly disabled person in need of a wheelchair ramp. If you can find a willing craftsperson who knows how to do the

Working as a volunteer on a construction team does more than build skills; it builds character, confidence, and relationships. And it is fun!

job, you might be able to put a crew together, meet the need, and gain some skills in the process. Of course, be sure to investigate your state's or locality's rules on minimum age requirements for teens doing specific types of work, and, above all, study and implement safety measures.

BUILD SOMETHING

Don't overlook small projects. Schools and community groups that put on plays and programs can often use help designing sets, constructing stages, and doing lighting. Consider building gifts for friends' birthdays instead of buying them. You can find books with step-by-step plans for making bookshelves, planter boxes, or doll beds. Move up to more complex projects, like a serving cart, a trellis for the garden, or a porch swing.

Once you master the techniques, try designing and building something on your own. Build something large or a bit complex, like a two-story dollhouse, a chicken coop, a doghouse, or a carport, for example. Remember the phases of construction: design, procurement, construction, and post-construction. You go through all these stages when you build something sizeable, gaining more skills than simply woodworking.

BUILD YOUR DIGITAL PORTFOLIO

Any skills you acquire or are taught and certified in should be documented on your résumé. Your résumé shows what qualifies you for a particular job. As you take classes, work on teams, and build things, you should be adding to your résumé, even if you won't need it for a long while. Create a working portfolio now and refine it over time.

Before the digital age, when people applied for a position they presented paper résumés detailing their abilities and experience. Today, job seekers use digital portfolios illustrating their

TINY HOUSES

The average North American house is about 2,500 square feet (232 square meters). Can you imagine moving into a 100- to 400-square foot (9 to 37 sq m) living space? People all over the United States are making the move to tiny houses. The reasons are many. The little structures are far less expensive to build and maintain than standard homes, and they use far less energy more efficiently. Many are on wheels, so they are mobile. Many people who live in small homes say they are quite comfortable. Made of the same materials as other houses, they typically have a living area, a bath, and a kitchen on the "ground floor" and a loft for sleeping. The tiny house movement is not just about cheaper or lower energy housing. It is part of a larger push to live more simply.

Interest in small (under 1000 sq. ft./93 sq m) and tiny houses (under 400 sq. ft./37 sq m) was sparked by an architect who designed them to house victims of Hurricane Katrina.

achievements. Digital portfolios contain audio, video, graphic, and text presentations of your skills and your work. Every time you accomplish anything related to construction or management, you need to preserve it in one of these formats and add it to your working portfolio.

What kinds of achievements go into a portfolio? Whatever demonstrates that you possess the knowledge and skills to be a CM. Remember the personal traits and abilities the job requires? Knowledge of construction, working well with others, leadership, problem solving, flexibility, calmness under pressure, and communication. Take pictures of your projects and describe your involvement in terms of these qualities. For example, if you helped build a Habitat for Humanity house, show a video of yourself working with other team members and talk about a problem you encountered and how you resolved it. Add a chart that depicts the details of the tasks you completed. If you remodeled a room, include a diagram of your design plan and explain why you selected the colors or materials you used. In other words, don't just show what you did; demonstrate that you have what it takes to do whatever a boss may ask of you.

When you are a construction manager, your boss will ask a great deal of you. You will be expected to thoroughly understand every aspect of your project. You will be required to manage the people, materials, time, and money in such a way that the project is completed on time and under budget. You may be asked to solve problems you have never encountered before. Your boss might expect you to work long hours under difficult conditions.

The job of construction manager is very demanding, but it is also very rewarding. You will be able to see someone's dream translated from a drawing on paper to a tangible reality. And you will have the thrill of knowing that you were an essential element in making that happen.

glossary

accredited Recognized by some official body as meeting requirements for academic excellence.

apprentice Person who learns a craft by working for or with someone who is experienced at that craft.

blueprint A drawing, usually in blue ink, of an architect's plan for a building.

civil engineering Branch of engineering concerned with the design and construction of public works—roads, canals, dams, etc.

condominium Unit in a multi-unit building that is owned rather than rented; an apartment that someone owns.

construction technology Study of the materials and techniques used in building structures.

general contractor Person or company responsible for fulfilling the terms of a contract. Often used to mean a person who is self-employed as a manager and tradesperson and hires subcontractors.

glazier Construction craftsperson who cuts and installs glass.

green collar Having to do with environmentally friendly work. A white-collar worker works in an office, a blue-collar worker has a physical job, and a green-collar worker has a job concerned with conserving the environment.

HVAC Acronym for "heating, ventilation, and air-conditioning," a subset of the skilled trades.

internship A form of training in which a person works in a professional job under supervision and usually as an assistant to the supervisor.

journeyman Craftsperson, male or female, who has worked as an apprentice in a particular trade and has become certified or otherwise recognized as a competent worker in the trade

mechanical engineering Branch of engineering concerned with the design, construction, and use of machines in industry or building.

procurement The process of obtaining something. In construction, procurement refers not just to buying materials, but everything involved in getting them, including researching, finding suppliers, writing contracts, arranging for delivery, and paying for the materials.

professional Person who has received certification from an organization recognized as a body that sets standards for a specific job. The certification acknowledges that the person has met the educational and practice requirements to do the job.

subcontractor Person or company agreeing (by signing a contract) to perform some work for a company that has a contract to get the work done. Often abbreviated to "sub."

surveyor Person who measures various dimensions of land.

sustainable building Method of planning and construction that conserves and restores renewable resources and has as little negative impact on the environment as possible.

technician Person who specializes in the technical details of a particular occupation.

union Organization of people who work in a specific trade or craft.

for more information

American Institute of Constructors
700 N. Fairfax Street, Suite 510
Alexandria, VA 22314
(703) 683-4999
Website: http://professionalconstructor.site-ym.com
The American Institute of Constructors is a society of professional constructors. It establishes quality standards for the
   profession, provides continuing education, and certifies
   people who meet its standards for ethics and practice.

Building Futures for Youth
260 Brownlow Avenue, Unit 3
Dartmouth, NS B3B 1V9
Canada
(902) 468-2267 ext. 712
Website: http://www.buildingfutures.ca
Building Futures for Youth is a partnership of several
   Canadian organizations and businesses that help young
   people get started in the construction trades. It provides
   information on construction-related careers and
   apprenticeships.

Canadian Apprenticeship Forum
404-2197 Riverside Drive
Ottawa, ON K1H 7X3
Canada
(613) 235-4004
Website: http://caf-fca.org
The Canadian Apprenticeship Forum is a national nonprofit
   organization that promotes apprenticeship. Its Careers in

Trade program provides information, resources, and practical links about apprenticeships.

Construction Management Association of America
7926 Jones Branch Drive, Suite 800
McLean, VA 22102-3303
(703) 356-2622
Website: https://cmaanet.org
The Construction Management Association of America is an organization of professional construction and program managers in public and private sectors and academic institutions. It provides training and certification in construction management.

Habitat for Humanity International
121 Habitat Street
Americus, GA 31709-3498
(800) 422-4828
Website: http://www.habitat.org
Habitat for Humanity is an international nonprofit organization that mobilizes volunteers to build and repair houses for people who need help in obtaining safe, affordable housing.

National Electrical Contractors Association
3 Bethesda Metro Center, Suite 1100
Bethesda, MD 20814
(301) 657-3110
Website: http://www.necanet.org
The National Electrical Contractors Association is an association of professionals in the electrical contracting industry. It has student chapters and offers information about schools with construction management programs, apprenticeships, and career development.

U.S. Department of Labor
200 Constitution Avenue NW
Washington, DC 20210
(866) 487-2365
Website: http://www.dol.gov/apprenticeship
The U.S. Department of Labor provides information and
resources on careers, job training, and locations of jobs.
The website has links to job centers and training programs
throughout the country.

WEBSITES

Because of the changing nature of Internet links, Rosen
Publishing has developed an online list of websites related to
the subject of this book. This site is updated regularly. Please
use this link to access the list:

http://www.rosenlinks.com/ECAR/Manage

for further reading

Byers, Ann. *Jobs as Green Builders and Planners*. New York, NY: Rosen Publishing Group, 2010.

Deitshe, Scott. *Green-Collar Jobs: Environmental Careers for the 21st Century*. Santa Barbara, CA: Praeger, 2010.

Fehl, Pamela. *Business and Construction*. New York, NY: Facts On File, 2010.

Ferguson Publishing. *Careers in Focus: Construction*. New York, NY: Facts On File, 2010.

Gladwell, Stephen. *Construction Managers: Job Hunting—A Practical Manual for Job Seekers and Career Changers*. Emereo, 2012.

Henderson, Holley. *Becoming a Green Building Professional: A Guide to Careers in Sustainable Architecture, Design, Engineering, Development, and Operations*. Hoboken, NJ: John Wiley and Sons, 2012.

Institute for Career Research. *Career as an Electrician: Electrical Contractor*. Charleston, SC: Create Space, 2015.

Institute for Career Research. *Careers in Construction Contracting*. Charleston, SC: Create Space, 2014.

Jackson, Barbara J. *Construction Management Jump Start: The Best First Step Toward a Career in Construction Management*. Second edition. Indianapolis, IN: Wiley, 2010.

McKeon, John K. *Becoming a Construction Manager*. Hoboken, NJ: John Wiley and Sons, 2011.

Miller, Malinda. *Green Construction: Creating Energy-Efficient, Low Impact Buildings*. Broomall, MD: Mason Crest, 2010.

Niver, Heather Moore. *Careers in Construction*. New York, NY: Rosen Publishing Group, 2013.

Tishman, John, and Tom Shachtman. *Building Tall: My Life*

and the Invention of Construction Management. Ann Arbor, MI: University of Michigan Press, 2011.

Waldrup, Lee W. *Becoming an Architect: A Guide to Careers in Design.* Third edition. Hoboken, NJ: John Wiley and Sons, 2014.

bibliography

Career Overview. "Construction Management Careers, Jobs and Employment Information." Retrieved April 28, 2015 (http://www.careeroverview.com/construction-management-careers.html).

Duger, Rose. "CANstruction Program in Kearny Nears 100,000 Cans for Local Food Pantries." *Jersey Journal,* January 8, 2015. Retrieved May 17, 2015 (http://www.nj.com/hudson/index.ssf/2015/01/canstruction_program_in_kearny_nears_100000_cans_for_local_food_pantries.html).

Helmer, Matt, Amy Blair, and Allison Gerber. *A Solid Foundation: Key Capacities of Construction Pre-Apprenticeship Programs.* Aspen Institute, 2012. Retrieved May 13, 2015 (http://www.aspenwsi.org/wordpress/wp-content/uploads/aspen_construction_WEB.pdf).

Home Building Answers. "Construction Project Scheduling: The Planning Phase." Retrieved April 29, 2015 (http://www.home-building-answers.com/construction-project-scheduling.html).

Institution of Structural Engineers. "World's First 'Passive-House' Skyscraper." March 9, 2013. Retrieved May 12, 2015 (http://www.istructe.org/news-articles/2013/industry-newsworld-s-first-passive-house%E2%80%9D-skyscraper?feed=Latest-News-Features).

iSeek.org. "Construction Project Manager Interview: Joanna Slominski." Retrieved April 29, 2015 (https://www.iseek.org/industry/green/careers/construction-project-manager.html).

Leir, Ron. "Can-do Attitude for Kearny High School 'Canstruction' projects." *Observer,* May 23, 2012.

Retrieved May 17, 2015 (http://www.theobserver.com/20
12/05/%E2%80%98can%E2%80%99-do-attitude-for-
kearny-high-school%E2%80%98canstruction%E2%80%
99-projects).

My Footpath. "Construction Management Interview: Ryan
Nellis." Retrieved May 11, 2015 (http://myfootpath.com/
career-advice-and-answers/career-interviews/construction-
management-career-interview/#sthash.ExjGeMPJ.dpuf).

Passipedia. "What Is a Passive House?" Retrieved May 11,
2015 (http://passipedia.passiv.de/ppediaen/basics/
what_is_a_passive_house).

PayScale. "Project Manager, Construction." Retrieved April 2,
2015 (http://www.payscale.com/research/US/Job=Project_
Manager,_Construction/Salary).

Restoring Simple. "Tiny House Statistics." Retrieved May 17,
2015 (http://restoringsimple.com/our-tiny-house/
tiny-house-statistics).

San Francisco Building and Construction Trades Council.
"Building Trades Craft Unions Offer Apprenticeship
Programs." Retrieved May 13, 2015 (http://www.sfbuild-
ingtradescouncil.org/apprentice-programs).

U.S. Department of Labor, Bureau of Labor Statistics.
Occupational Outlook Handbook, 2014–2015. Retrieved
April 6, 2015 (http://www.bls.gov/ooh).

U.S. Department of Labor, Employment and Training
Administration. Apprenticeship USA. Retrieved May 4,
2015 (http://www.doleta.gov/oa/apprenticeship.cfm).

U.S. Green Building Council. "Green Building Facts."
Retrieved May 12, 2015 (http://www.usgbc.org/articles/
green-building-facts).

U.S. Green Building Council. *LEED for New Construction
Reference Guide* (Version 2.2). Washington, DC: U.S.
Green Building Council, 2005.

U.S. Green Building Council. *LEED for New Construction*

Reference Guide, Version 2.2. 3rd edition. 2005. Retrieved May 11, 2015 (http://www.usgbc.org/Docs/Archive/General/Docs3179.pdf).

index

ABOUT THE AUTHOR

Ann Byers is a youth worker who has helped high school students and young adults learn life skills. For this book she consulted with Orville Williams, a construction company owner, and Cory Walczak, a construction manager.

PHOTO CREDITS

Cover, p 1 (figure), pp. 14-15 © iStockphoto.com/shotbydave; cover (background) Zurijeta/Shutterstock.com; p. 4 Andresr/Shutterstock.com; pp. 8-9 Kunal Mehta/Shutterstock.com; p. 10 Peter Cade/The Image Bank/Getty Images; p. 12 © Botastock images/Alamy Stock Photo; p. 16 Eudald Castells/Moment/Getty Images; p. 19 Lawrence Migdale/Science Source/Getty Images; pp. 22-23 Fuse/Thinkstock; p. 25 Juanan Barros Moreno/Shutterstock.com; p. 27 © iStockphoto.com/pastorscott; pp. 30-31 Kletr/Shutterstock.com; p. 33 Marina Lohrbach/Shutterstock.com; p. 34 Nagy-Bagoly Arpad/Shutterstock.com; pp. 36-37 Jozef Sowa/Shutterstock.com; p. 39 © Blend Images/Alamy Stock Photo; pp. 42-43 gpointstudio/Shutterstock.com; p. 45 sanjeri/E+/Getty Images; p. 49 © iStockphoto.com/lisafx; p. 51 © iStockphoto.com/skynesher; pp. 52-53 Michael Blann/Digital Vision/Getty Images; p. 57 Maximilian Stock Ltd./The Image Bank/Getty Images; p. 59 Tommaso Tagliaferri/E+/Getty Images; pp. 60-61 Hero Images/Getty Images; p. 63 Susan Law Cain/Shutterstock.com

Designer: Matt Cauli; Editor/Photo Researcher: Philip Wolny